P9-DEL-755

# DINOSAURS

Written by Rupert Matthews

Illustrations by Alex Head-Weston, Sarah Lever,
John Butler & Robert Morton

TOP THAT! Kids™

# TERRIBLE LIZARD

**Dinosaurs are among the most amazing creatures to have ever walked on Earth. Some dinosaurs looked very strange indeed. Some had spikes, some had frills, and some had crests. Ever since the first dinosaur remains were discovered, they have been famous. Movies have been made about dinosaurs and hundreds of books written about them.**

*When a dinosaur dies...*

*...it eventually becomes buried...*

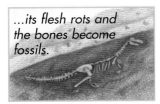

*...its flesh rots and the bones become fossils.*

## What were dinosaurs

Dinosaurs were reptiles which lived on Earth many millions of years ago. Scientists divide reptiles into groups based on the shape of their skulls. Dinosaurs belonged to the group of reptiles called diapsid. Scientists, called palaeontologists, learn about dinosaurs by digging fossils out of the ground. When an animal dies, the bones, teeth, and other pieces may become buried and preserved.

*A palaeontologist at work.*

## Why are they called "dinosaurs"

When the first dinosaur fossils were found, scientists did not know what they were. They thought the fossils belonged to very large lizards. Scientists often use Greek or Latin words to describe new discoveries. The word "dinosaur" is Greek for "terrible lizard." Scientists also use Greek or Latin to name types of animal. In the case of dinosaurs, the words chosen often describe something unusual about the dinosaur's body, the place where it was found, its behavior, or the person who discovered it.

## Where did dinosaurs live

Dinosaurs lived on every continent on Earth. They lived in forests, among hills, and in swamps. Wherever you live, the surrounding area was once home to dinosaurs. You would not recognize the continents that they lived on as they have changed in shape over time. Dinosaurs lived a very long time ago in a period scientists call the Mesozoic Era. The Mesozoic Era began about 245 million years ago and ended about 65 million years ago.

| TRIASSIC 245–208 million years | JURASSIC 208–146 million years | CRETACEOUS 146–65 million years |
|---|---|---|

← MESOZOIC ERA →

*A pterosaur in mid-flight. Pterosaurs were flying reptiles living around the time of the dinosaurs.*

## How many types ❓

Scientists have found at least 700 different types of dinosaur. There are many fossils which have not yet been dug out of the ground. There are probably hundreds of other types of dinosaur which have not yet been discovered. Dinosaurs came in many different shapes and sizes. Some dinosaurs were as small as a modern chicken. Others were larger than a bus, or even a house!

## How is a dinosaur special ❓

Dinosaurs are different from other reptiles in several ways. The legs of most reptiles stick out sideways from the body, whereas dinosaurs' were held directly underneath, giving them a more fluid movement. Let's not forget their size—no mammal, including the blue whale, has ever matched them for sheer bulk.

## Could dinosaurs fly ❓

None of the dinosaurs that have been discovered so far were able to fly. At the time of the dinosaurs there were flying reptiles which looked rather like modern bats. These are known as pterosaurs, which means "wing reptiles."

### FACT BYTES

There are no dinosaurs alive on Earth today. Some movies show dinosaurs fighting with humans, but they are wrong. All the dinosaurs died out millions of years ago.

So far, no dinosaurs have been found that lived in the sea. There were giant sea reptiles, but these were not dinosaurs. These animals included plesiosaurs and ichthyosaurs.

## TERRIBLE LIZARD

# FEEDING HABITS

Different dinosaurs ate different sorts of food. Some dinosaurs ate meat, others ate plants, and at least one type of dinosaur ate fish. Scientists study the fossil teeth of dinosaurs to decide what sort of food they ate when they were alive.

## How big were dinosaur teeth ❓

The size of dinosaur teeth varied. Small dinosaurs generally had very small teeth. The largest dinosaur teeth belonged to the giant hunter Giganotosaurus (right). One tooth was over 10 in. long and was very sharp. Several dinosaurs had no teeth at all. These are called ornithomimosaurs (below), which means "bird-like reptiles." They got this name because they looked rather like modern ostriches. Nobody knows what these dinosaurs ate. They may have fed on fruit or insects, and some scientists think they may have eaten eggs of other dinosaurs.

## Why did dinosaurs have claws ❓

Hunting dinosaurs had strong, sharp claws. They used the claws to attack other dinosaurs. Plant-eating dinosaurs also had claws, but these were short and blunt, and helped grip the ground as they walked.

## Which dinosaur ate fish ❓

Scientists found a fossilized fish inside the stomach of Baryonyx. This shows that Baryonyx ate fish. The teeth of Baryonyx were long and very sharp. This made them ideal for catching slippery fish.

*Baryonyx lived on a staple diet of fish.*

## How much did dinosaurs eat

Some dinosaurs ate huge meals. A giant such as Brachiosaurus might have eaten over 200 pounds of food every day. This might explain the fact that scientists have found huge pieces of fossilized dinosaur excrement. Some pieces were over 20 in. long!

Some plant-eating dinosaurs ate stones and pieces of rock. The stones were kept in the stomach of the dinosaur. If the animal ate tough plants, the rocks would pound the food into mush so that it could be more easily digested.

*Some dinosaurs ate stones to aid digestion.*

## How did dinosaurs hunt

Scientists think that the hunting dinosaurs may have used different tactics to get their food. Big hunting dinosaurs, such as Allosaurus, hunted alone because they were big enough to kill prey on their own. Other dinosaurs, such as Deinonychus, may have hunted in packs. It would have taken several Deinonychus to bring down a large victim.

### FACT BYTES

Most meat-eating (carnivorous) dinosaurs ate other dinosaurs. They hunted plant-eating (herbivorous) dinosaurs for food.

Some types of hunter ate other hunting dinosaurs. In fact, Coelophysis even ate other Coelophysis—friendly, huh!

**FEEDING HABITS**

# LIFESTYLE

**Nobody has ever seen a living dinosaur. Scientists cannot go to watch a dinosaur in the wild to see how it lives. Instead, they look at the dinosaur fossils and compare them to modern animals. Scientists also study other evidence such as fossilized tracks. Together these give many clues as to how dinosaurs lived.**

## How did dinosaurs reproduce ?

Dinosaurs laid eggs, from which young dinosaurs later hatched. Dinosaur eggs were very similar to modern bird eggs. They had a hard shell on the outside to protect them from damage. Inside, each had a yolk to provide food and albumen to supply water. The baby dinosaur grew inside the egg until it was large enough to hatch. Dinosaurs are thought to have piled leaves and twigs on top of their nests to keep the eggs warm. As the vegetation slowly rotted, it gave off heat. Dinosaurs which looked after their nests may have added or taken away leaves to keep the eggs at a steady temperature.

## How large were dinosaur eggs ?

Different dinosaurs laid eggs of varying sizes. The largest dinosaurs laid eggs that were larger than a modern basketball and were almost perfectly round. These very big eggs belonged to sauropod dinosaurs. Smaller dinosaur eggs were often oval. They could be smaller than a golf ball.

*Dinosaurs kept their nests warm with leaves and twigs.*

## Where did dinosaurs build their nests

Most dinosaurs laid their eggs in nests. Some nests were buried underground in soft earth so that predators could not find them. Other dinosaurs stayed close to their nests and guarded them. These nests were above ground and may have been in the open. No dinosaur built a nest in water, as this would have killed the babies.

*A few of the dinosaur types had large crests of bone or flaps of skin. These included (from top) Triceratops, Pachycephalosaurus, Parasaurolophus, and Torosaurus.*

## Why did dinosaurs have crests ❓

Some types of dinosaur had large crests of bone or flaps of skin on their heads and necks. These may have been covered in brightly colored skin. The dinosaur would have used these to send signals to other dinosaurs. The signals might have warned of danger or told others to stay away or to attract a mate. They also gave off other "warning" signals.

## What sounds did dinosaurs make ❓

Some dinosaurs were probably able to communicate through deep, rumbling calls. An amazingly well preserved Allosaurus has enabled scientists to compare the region of the brain associated with sound to that of its closest living relative, the crocodile. This has led to the conclusion that Allosaurus, and similar dinosaurs, probably made low-frequency sounds just like the crocodiles of today.

## What did baby dinosaurs eat ❓

Some types of plant-eating dinosaurs brought food to their babies in the nest. The parents gathered leaves and may have chewed them first to make them easier for the young to digest. Other dinosaurs did not feed their babies, so the young had to find their own food as soon as they hatched.

### FACT BYTES

Some plant-eating dinosaurs lived in groups called herds. The young dinosaurs stayed in the middle of the group. This meant that the large adults could protect the young from predatory hunting dinosaurs.

# FAMILY TREES

All dinosaurs belonged to one of two groups, divided according to the shape of their hip bones. One group is called the saurischia, meaning "lizard-hipped." The other group is the ornithischia, meaning "bird-hipped." Within each large group are several families of dinosaurs which contain animals which were fairly alike.

## What were the saurischia ?

The lizard-hipped dinosaurs had hip bones shaped like those of a modern lizard. All meat-eating dinosaurs were saurischia. The sauropod dinosaurs were saurischia, too. These were the dinosaurs with long necks and long tails. The saurischia included both the largest and the smallest dinosaurs.

**Ilium**

**Ischium**

**Pubis**

The hip bone of the saurischia.

## What were the ornithischia ?

The bird-hipped ornithischia dinosaurs had hip bones shaped like those of modern birds. All ornithischia were plant-eaters. Some bird-hipped dinosaurs had horns, crests, bone plates, and other strange growths on their heads or bodies. Interestingly, birds are believed to have evolved from the saurischians rather than the ornithischians!

**Ilium**

**Ischium**

**Pubis**

The hip bone of the ornithischia.

The Eoraptor is one of the earliest known dinosaurs.

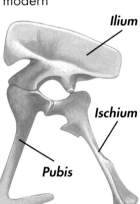

## Which was the first dinosaur ?

Perhaps the earliest known dinosaur was Eoraptor. This meat-eating dinosaur belonged to the saurischia group. It was about 10 feet long. Eoraptor lived 230 million years ago in South America. A "missing link" may have existed at the same time, which was a reptile that was the common ancestor of the ornithischia and the saurischia dinosaurs. No scientist has ever found a fossil of this animal.

## What were the dinosaur families ?

Scientists try to group dinosaurs into families, members of whom share features in common. Those that share common ancestors form groups called clades, and this classification method is known as cladistics. It may also help paleontologists to predict as-yet-unknown dinosaurs. This diagram shows the main families and how they were related. Dinosaurs often take their name from their most distinctive features, often in the Latin or Ancient Greek form. Some are named after the people who discovered them or after the place in which they were found.

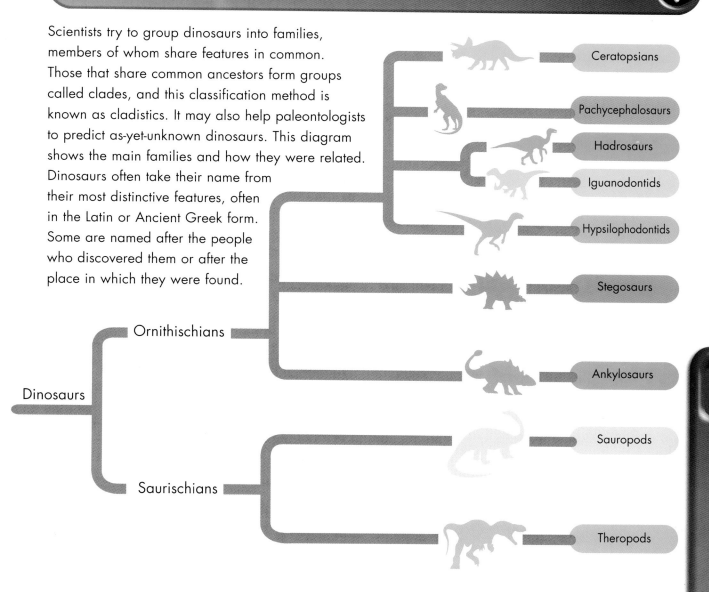

Ceratopsians

Pachycephalosaurs

Hadrosaurs

Iguanodontids

Hypsilophodontids

Stegosaurs

Ornithischians

Ankylosaurs

Dinosaurs

Sauropods

Saurischians

Theropods

## Did all dinosaurs live at the same time ?

The dinosaurs lived on Earth for around 170 million years. During that long period of time, many different types of dinosaur evolved, and some died out. For example, Stegosaurus had been extinct for 80 million years before Tyrannosaurus came on the scene. Some entire families died out during this time, and several new families appeared just before the dinosaurs became extinct. All dinosaurs adapted certain methods in order to survive during their periods of existence.

### FACT BYTES

The plant-eating dinosaurs all had different ways of defending themselves—this might include the development of armor plating on their bodies, horns on their faces, or spikes on their hands.

# THEROPODS

All the theropods were meat-eating dinosaurs. Most of them hunted other types of dinosaurs, although a few fed on insects, fish, or other small animals. The word theropod means "beast foot." The hind legs of all theropods had three toes pointing forwards, each of which had a sharp claw.

## Why did theropods walk on their hind legs ?

Theropods hunted other animals for food. They needed to be fast, strong, and agile. By using only their hind legs for walking theropods could run quickly. The long tail balanced the weight of the head and body. Theropods could change direction suddenly by jerking their tails to one side. Theropods did not need to walk on their front legs, so the limbs evolved to do other things instead. Most theropods had three "fingers," each with a sharp claw used to attack their prey. A few theropods had tiny front legs which would have been almost useless.

## When did theropods live ?

Theropods lived from the mid-Triassic period until the end of the Cretaceous period. Their fossils have been found all over the world, so we can assume that they were widespread.

| TRIASSIC 245–208 million years | JURASSIC 208–146 million years | CRETACEOUS 146–65 million years |
| --- | --- | --- |

## How did theropods find food ?

Nearly all theropods ate meat. Most theropods hunted for food by catching and killing other dinosaurs. Some theropods scavenged instead of hunting. This means that they looked for animals which had already died from disease or old age.

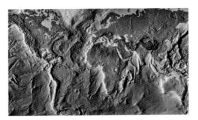

## How did the Deinonychus kill prey ?

The name of the dinosaur Deinonychus means "terrible-claw." It was given this name because of the weapon on its hind foot. The claw was about 5 in. long. Deinonychus was around 12 feet long. The killing weapon was a sharp, curved claw which was attached to the first toe on each foot. The toe was powered by strong muscles. Deinonychus could kick at prey, flicking its terrible claw forwards and down. Few dinosaurs could survive an attack from this animal.

## What was the oddest therapod ❓

The Therinzinosaurus was unlike any other dinosaur. The front legs of this dinosaur were over 8 feet long and were powered by strong muscles. Each ended with three massive 2 feet long claws. The claws were curved and extremely sharp. None of the scientists who have studied Therinzinosaurus are certain what the claws were used for, nor how the dinosaur lived.

*Strong neck muscles to support the head.*

*The tail possibly acted as some kind of balance for the therapods.*

*Each foot was powered by strong muscles.*

*Each claw was about 5 in. long and was very useful in a fight.*

*The Therinzinosaurus (top) and Deinonychus (bottom).*

## How fast could they move ❓

The Struthiomimus was the fastest dinosaur of all. It had very long, muscular hind legs and was able to bound across the ground very quickly. It may have been able to reach speeds of around 30 mph— as fast as a modern race horse.

### FACT BYTES

Many of the smaller theropods were covered with feathers. It is thought that the feathers kept them warm. About 160 million years ago one type of feathered theropod evolved into birds. Some people call birds "living dinosaurs."

# SAUROPODS

The largest dinosaurs of all were the sauropods. These huge plant-eating dinosaurs lived in every area of the world. They were among the first dinosaurs to appear and were numerous during the Jurassic Period, between 208 and 146 million years ago. In the Cretaceous Period, between 146 and 65 million years ago, the sauropods became rarer. Many of them died out completely.

## How did sauropods use their necks ?

Scientists who have studied sauropod necks have found that they were usually held forwards, not upright. Sauropods probably stood in one place when feeding. They used their long necks to reach all the plants across a wide area. When they had eaten everything in reach, the sauropods would move forwards. This allowed them to eat a large amount of food without using up much energy. The tails of sauropods were very long to enable them to balance their long necks. The longest neck of any dinosaur—at about 40 feet long— belonged to Mamenchisaurus.

## What did sauropods eat ?

Sauropods ate plants. Scientists studying sauropod teeth believe that these dinosaurs ate leaves from trees and bushes and fern fronds.

## When did sauropods live ?

Sauropods appeared in the late Triassic period with many different types becoming widespread by the Jurassic period. They become extinct at the end of the Cretaceous period. Fossils have been found on all continents except Antarctica.

| TRIASSIC 245–208 million years | JURASSIC 208–146 million years | CRETACEOUS 146–65 million years |
|---|---|---|

*The Seismosaurus had a very long neck which may have enabled it to reach tree tops.*

## How did sauropods swim ?

Scientists have found prints left by a sauropod swimming across a lake. It used the water to support its body and pushed itself along with its front legs. When it wanted to change direction, the sauropod kicked the lake bottom with a hind foot.

*The Argentinosaurus had backward-pointing neck vertebrae. This type of sauropod is known as a "low-level feeder."*

## Why were sauropods so large ?

Sauropods grew to be so large because this made them safer from attack by hunting dinosaurs. Even the largest hunter was only a tenth as large as an adult sauropod. They were able to grow to this size because there was enough food for them to eat and because they lived on open plains where there were no trees or steep hills to get in their way.

### FACT BYTES

Sauropods were huge creatures, but they had small brains. The average sauropod had a brain about the same size as that of a modern cat. Sauropods were probably not very clever.

SAUROPODS

13

# ANKYLOSAURS

The ankylosaurs were armored dinosaurs, covered in plates of bone which grew in their skin. Some ankylosaurs had spikes and spines of bone as well as armor plate. Most were about 13 feet long and walked on all fours.

## How are the ankylosaurs divided

Scientists have divided the ankylosaurs into two families. The nodosaurids had bone armor across their back and often had spikes. The ankylosaurids had armor on their heads as well, and tails with clubs on.

## Which was found first

The first ankylosaur to be found by scientists was Hylaeosaurus. The fossils were found in southern England in 1833. They were studied by the scientist Richard Owen, who also had fossils of Iguanodon and Megalosaurus. He grouped them together and gave them the name "dinosaurs" in 1842.

### FACT BYTES

Ankylosaurs had small, blunt teeth. They probably ate plants that did not need to be chewed very much. Perhaps they ate fruit.

*Fierce-looking ankylosaurs with heavy body armor and protective spikes and clubs.*

## When did ankylosaurs live

The nodosaurids lived from the late Jurassic Period to the late Cretaceous Period and the ankylosaurids lived from the mid to late Cretaceous Period. They lived largely in the northern continents.

| TRIASSIC 245–208 million years | JURASSIC 208–146 million years | CRETACEOUS 146–65 million years |
|---|---|---|

## How did ankylosaurs use their noses ❓

Ankylosaurs had unusual noses. When an ankylosaur breathed in, the air entered the nostrils then passed through strange S-shaped tubes. Scientists think this warmed the air before it entered the lungs. Ankylosaurs could have lived in cold, mountainous places.

*The club at the end was formed from fused bone.*

*Sharp spines protected the body.*

## Were ankylosaurs vulnerable ❓

Ankylosaurs were the "tanks" of the dinosaur world. The only way an ankylosaur could really be hurt was if it was flipped over. Its soft under-belly was the only part of its body that was unprotected, but in order to get even close, any predator had to get past the defensive armor first.

## What was Polacanthus ❓

Polacanthus was a nodosaurid which lived in Britain about 125 million years ago. This means it lived in the same place at the same time as Hylaeosaurus. Scientists have found only the front half of Hylaeosaurus and the back half of Polacanthus. Its possible that the two dinosaurs are really the same creature.

# CERATOPSIANS

**The name ceratopsian means "horn face." Most ceratopsians had long, sharp horns growing from their faces or the back of their skulls.**

## When did ceratopsians live ?

Ceratopsians were one of the last dinosaur families to evolve. They were most numerous between 80 and 65 million years ago, at the end of the Cretaceous Period. The vast majority of Ceratopsians lived in western North America, and a few types lived in eastern Asia.

| TRIASSIC  245–208 million years | JURASSIC  208–146 million years | CRETACEOUS  146–65 million years |
|---|---|---|

## What did ceratopsians eat ?

Ceratopsians were plant eaters. The front of their mouths had no teeth, but had a beak rather like that of a modern parrot. Behind the beak were sharp, slicing teeth. Scientists think ceratopsians ate tough leaves, such as palm leaves, which were sliced into tiny pieces and then swallowed.

## What was the first ceratopsian ?

The first ceratopsian was Psittacosaurus, which lived about 95 million years ago in Asia. Like most small plant-eating dinosaurs it walked on its hind legs and used its "hands" to hold food. Psittacosaurus had the same beak and teeth as later ceratopsians. Psittacosaurus was about six feet long.

*The Psittacosaurus had a beak similar to that of a modern parrot.*

## How did ceratopsians fight ?

Scientist have found injuries on ceratopsian skulls caused by horns of other ceratopsians. It is thought that ceratopsians locked horns and wrestled with each other much as modern deer lock antlers. These fights decided which ceratopsian would lead the herd.

## Which ceratopsian had the largest horns

Most ceratopsians had either one or three horns pointing forwards. Styracosaurus had just one horn pointing forwards, but it also had horns growing from the back of its skull.

Styracosaurus had nine horns in all. The horns of Torosaurus were over 4 feet long. Torosaurus also had the largest skull of any land animal which has ever lived. The skull was over 8 feet long.

*The Styracosaurus had one horn pointing forwards, but also had many others growing from the back of its skull.*

## Why did ceratopsians have large frills

Most ceratopsians had a frill of bone growing back from the rear of their skull. If they wagged their heads from side to side, the frill would have made a good display. Ceratopsians may have used these frills to frighten off rivals or hunting dinosaurs.

# ORNITHOPODS

**The ornithopods were a large group of plant-eating dinosaurs. There were several families of dinosaurs within the ornithopod group. The name ornithopod means "bird-foot." The group was given this name because some of the smaller ornithopods left tracks like modern birds.**

## When did the ornithopods live ?

The ornithopods lived throughout the age of the dinosaurs. Some of the earliest dinosaurs were ornithopods living in southern Africa about 215 million years ago. These were also the first ornithischia dinosaurs. Various types of ornithopod lived up until 65 million years ago.

| TRIASSIC  245–208 million years | JURASSIC  208–146 million years | CRETACEOUS  146–65 million years |
|---|---|---|

## What were the hadrosaurs ?

The hadrosaurs were a family of ornithopod dinosaurs which lived in North America and eastern Asia between 95 and 65 million years ago. They were larger than most ornithopods reaching between 20 and 43 feet.

## How did hadrosaurs communicate ?

Hadrosaurs had large crests of bone on top of their skulls. The crests varied in size and shape between different types of hadrosaur. Some of the crests were made of solid bone, other crests were hollow. The type of hadrosaurs with hollow crests were called "lambeosaurinae." They took in air through the top of the crest, which passed through nasal passages and chambers, breathing out of the nostrils and causing a loud "honk!" This could have been used as a way of attracting a mate.

Cross section through bone

Air chamber

Nasal passage

Meeting point of right and left nasal passages

Nostril

*Cross-section of a hadrosaur's skull.*

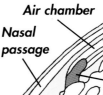

## How did hadrosaurs eat ?

Hadrosaurs had hundreds of teeth in their jaws. The teeth were arranged so that when the dinosaur closed its mouth to eat, the teeth rubbed against each other and turned their food to mush.

## What were the other types of ornithopod ?

*Hypsilophodontids, a type of ornithopod, stood on their rear legs in order to reach high-up branches.*

Iguanodontids were a family of ornithopods which lived between 140 and 65 million years ago. Most iguanodontids lived in Europe and North America, but some lived in Africa and Australia. Iguanodontids grew to be between 15 and 30 feet long.

Hypsilophodontids were small or medium ornithopods. They walked on their hind legs and used their front legs to hold onto plants while they bit off leaves and twigs. There were many types of hypsilophodontids living all over the world.

*Many types of hadrosaur had large crests of bone on top of their skulls.*

## What was Ouranosaurus' sail ?

The iguanodontid Ouranosaurus had a large flap of skin supported on thin bones growing along its back. Ouranosaurus may have used the skin of this so called sail to change its body temperature. If it stood in the Sun, the sail could have absorbed heat to warm up the whole animal.

### FACT BYTES

Perhaps the earliest of the ornithopods was Lesothosaurus, which lived in what is now the African country of Lesotho.

This dinosaur was less than 3 feet long and weighed under 20 pounds. It lived 215 million years ago.

# PACHYCEPHALOSAURS

In 1940, scientists discovered a strange dinosaur skull. It was made of very thick bone and was covered with bony lumps and spikes. Nobody knew what sort of dinosaur it had come from nor what it had looked like when alive. It was some time before other fossils were found. Now we know a lot about pachycephalosaurs.

## When, and where, did the pachycephalosaurs live ?

The first pachycephalosaur lived about 110 million years ago. The last dinosaur in the family lived about 65 million years ago. Different sorts of pachycephalosaurs existed during this time. The later types had even thicker skulls than the ones which survived earlier. Most of these dinosaurs lived in western North America and eastern Asia. More fossils of more types of pachycephalosaur have been found in these areas than anywhere else.

| TRIASSIC 245–208 million years | JURASSIC 208–146 million years | CRETACEOUS 146–65 million years |
|---|---|---|

## What does pachycephalosaur mean ?

When the first fossils of dinosaurs with thick skull bones were found, scientists called them Pachycephalosaurus, which means "thick-skull reptile." As other similar dinosaur fossils were found, the name was given to the entire dinosaur family—the pachycephalosaurs. It is thought that these dinosaurs used their thick skulls to fight each other. Rival dinosaurs may have charged at one another with their heads lowered. After several hits, the weaker one would give up.

## Did the head banging hurt ?

The thick skull bones would have protected the brain of the pachycephalosaurs when their heads banged together. The neck bones of the dinosaurs were shaped so that the impact did not damage their spines.

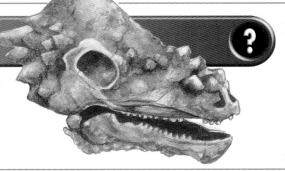

## How similar are they to animals today ❓

The modern bighorn sheep has a lifestyle very like that of pachycephalosaurs. When rival bighorn sheep fight over who will lead a herd they run at each other and bang their heads to prove which is the stronger animal. They live among mountains eating small plants, like the pachycephalosaurs who had fairly small and leaf-shaped teeth that would have been able to shred leaves.

### FACT BYTES

Scientists have found about twelve different types of pachycephalosaur, so far. It is believed that other types of this dinosaur family may still be buried in the ground.

## Why are pachycephalosaur fossils so rare ❓

Compared with other dinosaur fossils, those of pachycephalosaurs are very rare. Few of them are found and those that do occur are usually broken and have pieces missing. Scientists think that pachycephalosaurs may have lived in mountainous areas. Fossils do not form easily in these areas, so any animal living there would not leave much evidence.

*The thick, bony skulls of the pachycephalosaurs were probably used to ram attackers, used in displays of strength, and to impress the females in their group.*

# STEGOSAURS

**The stegosaurs are a family of ornithischian dinosaurs which lived all across Earth. The name means "roof-reptile," and refers to the large bone plates and spikes which run along the backs of many stegosaurs.**

## How many stegosaurs were there **?**

Scientists have found the fossils of about 20 types of stegosaur. All stegosaurs walked on all four legs, though some of them could rear up on their hind legs to reach food. The most famous type of stegosaur is the Stegosaurus—which is described in more detail on pages 38 and 39.

## When, and where, did the stegosaurs live **?**

The earliest stegosaurs lived about 165 million years ago. For the next 25 million years stegosaurs lived all across the world and the number of fossils shows they were quite common. Since 130 million years ago the stegosaurs began to become rarer, and died out around 100 million years ago. Stegosaurs have been found right across the world. The largest types lived in North America, while very few stegosaur fossils have been found in Africa or Australia.

### FACT BYTES

The smallest stegosaur found to date was the Kentrosaurus which was about 8 feet long.

Kentrosaurus had long bone spikes growing from its shoulders as well as along its back and tail.

| TRIASSIC 245–208 million years | JURASSIC 208–146 million years | CRETACEOUS 146–65 million years |
|---|---|---|

## What did stegosaurs eat **?**

Stegosaurs were plant eaters. Their teeth were small and sharp. At the time stegosaurs died out new types of plants were replacing older ferns and cycads. Perhaps stegosaurs ate the older sorts of plants and could not feed on the new types. This herbivore would have been preyed on by the fierce carnivore Allosaurus. Slow moving, they were an easy target.

## What was Tuojiangosaurus ?

This stegosaur lived in China about 145 million years ago. It had fifteen pairs of plates along its back and two pairs of long spikes on the end of its tail. Tuojiangosaurus grew to be about 23 feet long. Most of the rocks in the Far East are of a different age and very few dinosaur fossils have been found there.

*Many stegosaurs have large bone plates running along their backs.*

## When do we make mistakes ?

For many years, scientists thought that Dravidosaurus was a stegosaur that had survived in India for about 40 million years after they died out elsewhere. We now know that the bones of Dravidosaurus are really those of a sea reptile called a plesiosaur.

# COELOPHYSIS

**Coelophysis was a small, agile hunting dinosaur about 6 feet long. It had a long neck which it could twist and turn very quickly. This made it easier for Coelophysis to snap at food. It had long, muscular legs to help it chase after victims.**

## How many types of Coelophysis were there

When the first Coelophysis fossils were found in 1881, the scientist Edward Cope realized that there were three different types of animal. He decided they belonged to different species of Coelophysis. We now know that there was only one type of Coelophysis. The different skeletons had come from animals of different ages. They all had a very long, narrow head and jaws at the end of a long neck, and arms, with useful grasping "hands."

## What did Coelophysis eat ?

Coelophysis had a mouth full of short, but razor-sharp, teeth which meant it probably ate small animals, such as lizards. Coelophysis would have swallowed some of its victims whole, while others would have been sliced to pieces. Palaeontologists found a complete skeleton of an adult Coelophysis with two whole Coelophysis inside. They were too well formed to be embryos, so it is thought that Coelophysis sometimes ate their own young—they were cannibals!

*Coelophysis had four fingers on each "hand" but only three were strong enough to grasp prey.*

## When, and where, did the Coelopysis live ?

Coelophysis lived about 223 million years ago during the Triassic Period. At this time there were few other dinosaurs alive. Coelophysis was one of the earliest dinosaurs. The fossils of Coelophysis have been found in the southwestern part of North America. Similar dinosaurs lived at the same time, but Coelophysis lived in just one small area.

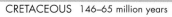

| TRIASSIC 245–208 million years | JURASSIC 208–146 million years | CRETACEOUS 146–65 million years |
|---|---|---|

←——————→

## When did Coelophysis go into space

Coelophysis has gone into space! In January 1998, NASA's Space Shuttle *Endeavour* linked the Triassic Period to the space age when it blasted off with a Coelophysis skull on board. Retired astronaut Jay Apt was in charge of the 215 million-year-old skull and persuaded the astronauts to take it into space with them. Although the skull wasn't used in any scientific tests, it did spend some time on the *Mir* space station before orbiting Earth and returning home safely.

## How did Coelophysis catch its prey

Some palaeontologists think that Coelophysis may have hunted in packs. This means that they probably had large brains in order to plan their hunts and would have been able to work together as a group, surrounding their unfortunate victims.

### FACT BYTES

Coelophysis means "hollow form." This dinosaur had light, hollow bones which meant it could run very fast. The average Coelophysis reached 10 feet in length.

## How many have been found

In 1947, scientists working for the American Museum of Natural History were digging in dinosaur-age rocks in New Mexico when they found hundreds of Coelophysis skeletons all piled up on top of one another. Scientists have never again found so many fossils all in the same place.

# ALLOSAURUS

Allosaurus was a large meat-eating dinosaur. It walked on its hind legs and attacked prey with its sharp front claws and powerful teeth. Allosaurus belongs to a group of dinosaurs called carnosaurs, which means "meat-reptiles."

## When, and where, did Allosaurus live ❓

Allosaurus lived about 150 million years ago, in the late Jurassic Period. Allosaurus lived in North America. Fossils have been found in Wyoming, Colorado and nearby areas. Very similar bones have been found in Portugal but scientists are unsure whether they are of the Allosaurus.

| TRIASSIC  245–208 million years | JURASSIC  208–146 million years | CRETACEOUS  146–65 million years |
| --- | --- | --- |

*A carnivorous dinosaur, the Allosaurus could capture its prey in its strong jaws.*

## What does it mean ❓

The name Allosaurus means "strange reptile." It was given this name because its skull is different from that of other hunting dinosaurs. There are a pair of bone ridges along the top of the skull and the internal layout of the skull bones is unique.

## How did allosaurs survive ❓

Scientists think that Allosaurus may have hidden among trees and then leapt out onto any plant-eating dinosaurs that came close enough. Allosaurus had dozens of teeth in its jaws. Although these teeth were of many different sizes, they were all curved so that the tips pointed backwards. This meant that once a victim was caught, it would find it almost impossible to wriggle free.

## Could Allosaurus run

Allosaurus was a very strong, but heavy, animal which grew to be about 45 feet in length and may have weighed around 4 tons. Scientists think that Allosaurus could not run very quickly, perhaps only about 6 mph, which most humans could beat. It was a strongly held theory that Allosaurus refrained from running as it only had little arms which could not break its fall. However, bone expert Dr. Bruce Rothschild has found evidence of fourteen fractured, but healed, ribs probably received when this huge, lumbering animal tripped and bellyflopped. This suggests that Allosaurus ran, fell over—and got back up again!

## Who missed a great find

In 1877, the fossil collector Benjamin Mudge was digging for fossils in an area of dinosaur-age rocks in Freemont County, Colorado. He found a few tail bones which he called Allosaurus, then gave up digging. In 1884, another collector named Othniel Marsh dug a bit deeper on the same spot and found an entire Allosaurus skeleton. Mudge had missed it by about 2 inches!

*Fossil collector Benjamin Mudge came within inches of discovering a complete Allosaurus.*

## What was the Chinese fossil

In 1978, Chinese scientists found the fossils of a dinosaur which was very similar to the Allosaurus of North America. This hunter was only about 20 feet long, but was otherwise almost the same as the American version. It is known as Yangchuanosaurus, as it was found near the town of Yang Chuan.

### FACT BYTES

After a huge meal, Allosaurus would have laid down to bask in the Sun!

Allosaurus had some thin, fragile ribs that helped protect its internal organs. Unusually, these were not attached to the backbone, but were fixed to the skin in the belly area.

ALLOSAURUS

# TYRANNOSAURUS REX

When the fossils of Tyrannosaurus were found in 1902, it was the largest hunter that had been unearthed. It was given the name Tyrannosaurus rex, which means "king of the tyrant reptiles."

## When, and where, did Tyrannosaurus rex live ?

Tyrannosaurus was one of the very last dinosaurs to walk on Earth. It lived about 66 million years ago at the end of the Cretaceous Period. Tyrannosaurus lived in the western part of North America. Similar dinosaur fossils have been found in eastern Asia and in South America.

| TRIASSIC 245–208 million years | JURASSIC 208–146 million years | CRETACEOUS 146–65 million years |
|---|---|---|

## How big was Tyrannosaurus rex ?

Tyrannosaurus was about 45 feet long and weighed around 6.5 tons. The skull was a huge 5 feet long. This made T-rex much larger than any other hunting dinosaur known when the fossils were found, and for 100 years afterward.

## How did Tyrannosaurus rex move around ?

Tyrannosaurus' stout legs did not support its heavy body very well, and would only be able to run at 12 mph. It probably hid, waited for prey to come along, and surprised it with a terrifying pounce. This method is known as "ambushing."

## How strong was the bite of Tyrannosaurus rex ?

*Tyrannosaurus rex's stomach could hold up to 500 pounds of meat.*

Tyrannosaurus had dozens of teeth and was constantly growing new ones to replace those that broke or fell out in fights. Each tooth was about 8 in. long and was serrated, like a steak knife, to cut through meat. The jaws of Tyrannosaurus were moved by powerful muscles attached to the top of its skull. Tyrannosaurus could snap its jaws shut with three times the force of a modern lion. It was able to crunch up bones and swallow them in pieces.

## Where can I see a skeleton of a real Tyrannosaurus rex ?

Sue Hendrickson was on a dig in South Dakota in 1990 when she discovered the largest and most complete T-Rex skeleton ever found. Named "Sue" in her honor, the bones were so well preserved that even the bones of the inner ear were still there! Sue was re-constructed using fake bones where some were missing, and is displayed at the Chicago Field Museum.

## What did Tyrannosaurus rex eat ?

Some scientists think that Tyrannosaurus moved so slowly that it could not catch any other dinosaurs. Perhaps Tyrannosaurus scavenged meat from dinosaurs which had died of disease or old age. It could have easily filled up on dead dinosaur—scientists think that a Tyrannosaurus was able to swallow as much as 500 pounds of meat and bone at once!

# COMPSOGNATHUS

The name Compsognathus means "pretty jaw." The dinosaur was given this name because its jaw was small, light, and the whole fossil was beautifully preserved. The fossil was so complete that scientists could see that it still had eggs inside it.

## When, and where, did Compsognathus live ?

Compsognathus lived about 155 million years ago toward the end of the Jurassic Period. Compsognathus lived in Europe. Its fossils have been found in southern Germany and in the south of France. Similar dinosaurs lived right around the world at the same time.

| TRIASSIC  245–208 million years | JURASSIC  208–146 million years | CRETACEOUS  146–65 million years |
| --- | --- | --- |

## How large was Compsognathus ?

Compsognathus was the smallest dinosaur so far discovered. It was only about 2 feet long and may have weighed around 5 pounds. This means Compsognathus was about the size of a modern chicken. However, its size did not mean it couldn't look after itself. Being so small, it could have run very fast and would easily be able to outrun the more lumbering dinosaurs!

## How did Compsognathus hunt ?

Compsognathus could run very quickly and was able to turn suddenly. It probably hunted small animals by dashing quickly from place to place, snapping victims up in its jaws. The teeth were small and very sharp, so it could have grabbed hold of fast moving targets. One fossilized Compsognathus was found with its last meal still inside it. This showed that Compsognathus ate lizards, but it probably hunted small mammals and large insects as well.

## How many types of Compsognathus were there ?

Scientists have found two types of Compsognathus. The first is known as Compsognathus longipes and is the type of fossil found in Germany. The fossils found in France are from a slightly larger animal and have been designated Compsognathus corallestris. Compsognathus was first discovered by the German scientist Dr. Obendorfer in 1857. Unfortunately, he forgot to write down exactly where he found the fossil, so other scientists have been unable to return to look for more.

*Compsognathus longipes.*

*Compsognathus corallestris.*

*Although small, Compsognathus could move quickly, catching its prey between sharp, pointed teeth.*

## Could Compsognathus swim ?

The Compsognathus corallestris from France had unusual front limbs. Although no fossil is complete, it is thought that the front limbs may have been equipped with broad flippers. These may have helped it to swim in lakes and lagoons.

### FACT BYTES

Compsognathus had two short arms, with two clawed fingers on each hand. Each foot included a tiny toe pointing backwards.

# GIGANOTOSAURUS

When the fossils of Giganotosaurus were first found, it was at once realized that they came from a very large hunter dinosaur. Scientists gave the new creature the name Giganotosaurus, which means "giant-southern-reptile."

## Who discovered Giganotosaurus ❓

Giganotosaurus fossils were found by Ruben Caroli in 1993 in a remote area of Neuquen in Patagonia, part of Argentina. The scientist Rodolfo Coria from the Carmen Funes Museum went to Neuquen to excavate the fossils and study them. The fossils of Giganotosaurus are kept in Argentina. However, plastic copies of the fossils have been made.

## When, and where, did Giganotosaurus live ❓

Giganotosaurus lived about 100 million years ago in the middle of the Cretaceous Period. Scientists did not find Giganotosaurus fossils until recently. The fossils of Giganotosaurus were found in 1993, and several other new types of dinosaur have been found in South America in recent years. Until the 1980s, there were few good roads in remoter parts of South America, so travel was very difficult. Scientists did not visit many areas so even though the fossils were there, nobody realized what they were.

| TRIASSIC 245–208 million years | JURASSIC 208–146 million years | CRETACEOUS 146–65 million years |
|---|---|---|

### FACT BYTES

The finding of this new dinosaur was kept secret for two years, then announced to the world in 1995.

## How large was Giganotosaurus ❓

When it was alive, Giganotosaurus measured about 50 feet long and stood 18 feet tall. It probably weighed around 7 tonnes. The skull was over 6 feet long, but, as is typical with very large dinosaurs, it had a small brain. Giganotosaurus was bigger and heavier than Tyrannosaurus rex, but had an even smaller brain—about the shape and size of a banana!

Banana sized brain.

*The Giganotosaurus was even larger than the mighty Tyrannosaurus rex.*

## What did Giganotosaurus eat ?

Giganotosaurus was a very large meat eater, like the Tyrannosaurus rex, and both preyed on plant-eating dinosaurs. However, whereas T-rex had long, wide teeth that varied in size, Giganotosaurus had shorter teeth of a more uniform size which were far better adapted to slicing flesh. There were lots of large plant-eaters around with which this beast could satisfy its appetite—and it is likely it briefly pursued its prey before inflicting fatal wounds with its mouth. To have an even greater chance of catching its food, Giganotosaurus may have preyed on young, isolated, or injured dinosaurs.

*Sharp, pointed teeth allowed Giganotosaurus to easily slice flesh off its prey.*

## Is Giganotosaurus still the king ?

The first fossils of a dinosaur named Carcharodontosaurus were found in Egypt at the beginning of the century. Written records of the find were made, and the fossils kept in Munich. However, the WWII bombings over the city destroyed the building and its contents. Modern-day palaeontologists were puzzled when they found a huge skull in the Sahara in 1995, but, as all the written evidence still existed from the earlier find, they were able to link it to the fossils that had been destroyed. Carcharodontosaurus was named the "shark-toothed reptile from the Sahara," and all the evidence points to it being at least as large as Giganotosaurus.

**GIGANOTOSAURUS**

# IGUANODON

**The name Iguanodon means "iguana-tooth." It was given to this dinosaur because its teeth look very like those of a modern iguana lizard, but they are much larger. This was the largest of the iguandontid dinosaurs and grew to be about 33 feet long.**

## When and where did Iguanodon live ❓

Iguanodon lived about 120 million years ago, near the beginning of the Cretaceous Period. Iguanodon lived in western Europe and eastern North America. Iguanodon fossils have also been found in parts of Asia and even Britain! Very similar animals lived in Africa and Australia. Iguanodon was the very first dinosaur to be discovered. Some fossilized teeth were found in Sussex by Dr. Gideon

Mantell in 1822. Mantell did not know what sort of animal the teeth came from but he knew they looked like teeth from the lizard iguana. Mantell thought Iguanodon must be a large, four-footed lizard.

*Long, pillar-like legs supported the Iguanodon's heavy body.*

| TRIASSIC  245–208 million years | JURASSIC  208–146 million years | CRETACEOUS 146–65 million years |
|---|---|---|

## What was the thumb spike for ❓

The Iguanodon thumb was equipped with a short, very sharp spike of bone. This may have been a weapon with which Iguanodon defended itself. It may have tried to stab an attacker with the thumb spike, which could inflict a nasty wound. It could also be used to find and scavenge food.

## How large was Iguanodon ❓

Iguanodon was about 30 feet long and could rear up on its back legs to over 15 feet in height. It stood just under 10 feet tall at the hips and may have weighed over 5 tons.

## How did Iguanodon chew its food

Iguanodon had jaws that slid sideways in the skull. This meant that every time it closed its mouth, the teeth would grind up anything between them. Iguanodon was able to grind food into tiny pieces ready to be swallowed and digested. At first scientists thought that all dinosaurs had mouths that opened all the way to the back of the jaw. Then they noticed that the jaws of Iguanodon had marks where cheeks had run along the side of the mouth.

**FACT BYTES**

As well as finding the Iguanodon teeth, Mantell found the remains of three other extinct creatures—a giant crocodile, a plesiosaur, and Megalosaurus.

## How did it move about

Scientists have found many sets of footprints belonging to the Iguanodon, and believe that it usually used all four "feet" to get around. It probably had thick back legs, and a pair of thin, light legs at the front. Rearing up on its back legs would have made it over 15 feet in height, and thus would have been an effective way of escaping from a predator's grasp. Its middle three "fingers" were joined together, but its little finger could move freely to grasp food.

## What was found at Bernissart

In 1878, men working a coal mine over 1,000 feet underground at Bernissart in Belgium found over 30 skeletons of Iguanodon mixed in with the coal. This was the first time that a complete dinosaur skeleton had been found!

**IGUANODON**

# BRACHIOSAURUS

When the scientist Elmer Riggs first found fossils of Brachiosaurus he realized it was a very unusual dinosaur. Nearly every other dinosaur had front legs shorter than its hind legs, but Brachiosaurus had short hind legs. As a result of this, Riggs gave the dinosaur the name Brachiosaurus, which means "arm-reptile." This giant weighed as much as twenty elephants!

## When, and where, did Brachiosaurus live ?

Brachiosaurus was alive during the late part of the Jurassic Period, about 150 million years ago. Brachiosaurus fossils have been found in North America and in East Africa. Very similar animals lived at about the same time in Africa and in eastern Asia.

| TRIASSIC 245–208 million years | JURASSIC 208–146 million years | CRETACEOUS 146–65 million years |
|---|---|---|

## How tall was Brachiosaurus ?

Brachiosaurus was one of the tallest dinosaurs. If it held its neck upright it would have stood 43 feet tall. It may have reached a total of 92 feet in length and weighed around 55 tons. The legs of this dinosaur had to bear all the weight of the body while moving. We refer to such creatures as "graviportal" or "heavy carrying"—like an elephant.

## What did Brachiosaurus eat

How could a dinosaur with such a small head take in enough food to fill its huge stomach? A Brachiosaurus would need to eat 500 pounds of food on a daily basis. Its nostrils could give us a clue. As they were placed high on the head, they would not interfere with the eating process—so it could munch almost continuously! It is thought that it used its long neck and high shoulders to reach to the tops of trees. Its peg-like teeth were useless for chewing, so it swallowed stones which broke down the tough fibers of the plants and turned them to mush in its stomach.

*Brachiosaurus swallowed stones which broke down the tough plant fibers into a digestible mushy soup.*

## Did Brachiosaurus live in water

When Brachiosaurus was found, scientists thought that the leg bones were not strong enough to have carried the weight of the dinosaur, and that Brachiosaurus and other sauropods must have lived in water which would have supported them. In addition, its nostrils were placed high on its forehead, suggesting that they could have been used a bit like a snorkel. While most scientists now agree that Brachiosaurus lived on land, there is evidence that they may have liked the water as their habitat featured low-lying plains bordered by an inland sea and crossed with rivers. Many remains have been found in these previously wet places.

## What's been the best find

In 1907, the German engineer W. Sattler noticed some enormous fossil bones while he was exploring Tendaguru, a remote part of Tanganyika. When he finished his exploration, Sattler happened to mention the fossils to Eberhard Fraas, who was interested in dinosaurs. Fraas realized the importance of the find and persuaded the German government to send an expedition. Over 275 tons of fossils were excavated, including a complete Brachiosaurus skeleton.

### FACT BYTES

The Brachiosaurus wouldn't have had much to fear. The largest known meat-eaters roaming about at the same time, Allosaurus and Ceratosaurus for example, weren't even half its size!

**BRACHIOSAURUS**

# STEGOSAURUS

**Stegosaurus is the largest and best known of the stegosaur family of dinosaurs. The first complete Stegosaurus skeleton was found in Wyoming in 1877 by Samuel Wendell Williston. Since then, other Stegosaurus fossils have been found. Stegosaurus was up to 30 feet long and stood 15 feet tall. It probably weighed over 2 tons.**

## When, and where, did Stegosaurus live  ?

Stegosaurus lived about 150 million years ago, towards the end of the Jurassic Period. Stegosaurus lived in the western parts of North America. Fossils have been found on several sites, so it probably ranged across a wide area. Animals similar to Stegosaurus lived in Africa, Europe, and Asia.

| TRIASSIC 245–208 million years | JURASSIC 208–146 million years | CRETACEOUS 146–65 million years |

## What was the purpose of the plates  ?

The large plates of bone that stood up from the back of Stegosaurus were covered by skin under which ran hundreds of veins carrying blood. It is thought that Stegosaurus could change its temperature using the plates. If it stood in the Sun, the blood would absorb heat and warm up the animal quickly. Some scientists think that Stegosaurus could change the color of the skin covering its plates. This would have made a dramatic display. Perhaps Stegosaurus used this to send signals to other Stegosaurus. It may have warned off rivals or sent warnings of danger.

## How many brains did the Stegosaurus have  ?

The skull of Stegosaurus is small and contained a tiny brain which is often described as being the "size of a walnut." Positioned in the backbone close to the hips was a second mass of nerve cells which weighed about 2 pounds. Some people think this was a second brain, but it was probably just a nerve center to work the legs and tail—the idea of it being a "relay junction box" is back in fashion.

## How did it defend itself ?

Stegosaurus was a large, heavy dinosaur. Its legs were solid and powerful and were built for strength, not for speed. Scientists think that Stegosaurus could not run at all. Instead it probably walked at about 5 mph. However, it had four long, sharp bone spikes on the end of its tail. The spikes were about two feet long. These were probably a defense against attack. If a hunter tried to attack Stegosaurus, the Stegosaurus would have lashed its tail from side to side to try to hit the hunter with its spikes.

*The distinctive Stegosaurus used its tail spikes when threatened or attacked.*

## FACT BYTES

It is unlikely that the plates would have protected Stegosaurus from an attack as they are not solid, but have honeycomb-like cavities (spaces) inside.

The back legs of a Stegosaurus were twice as long as its front legs and each toe had a hoof-like claw. Palaeontologists think that it walked on all four legs, but that it may have reared up to get hard-to-reach leaves.

## What did Stegosaurus eat ?

Stegosaurus was a plant eater. As its teeth were so small, it probably did not chew its food, but held it in its stomach until it was finally digested. This would have produced a lot of gas, which passed out with its droppings. Phew! It would have eaten the now-extinct members of the Cycad family— woody-stemmed, tough-leaved plants of the late Jurassic period.

*The Stegosaurus' stomach contents—its food would have remained in the stomach for days.*

**STEGOSAURUS**

# ANKYLOSAURUS

Ankylosaurus was the largest of the ankylosaurs. It was discovered in 1907 at about the same time as the remains of several other armored dinosaurs. There was much confusion about which fossils belonged to which type of armored dinosaur and it took many years for scientists to sort out the mixture.

## When, and where, did Ankylosaurus live ?

Ankylosaurus lived about 65 million years ago, at the end of the Cretaceous Period. Many fossils have been found at "Hell Creek"—a semi-arid region to the east of the Rockies in Montana. The area is frequently being exposed in the hunt for more fossils, and some of the very last of the dinosaurs have been found here, including T-rex.

*The Ankylosaurus' heavy armor of the body would put off an attacker, as they'd need to roll this dinosaur over to make it vulnerable!*

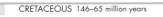

| TRIASSIC 245–208 million years | JURASSIC 208–146 million years | CRETACEOUS 146–65 million years |
|---|---|---|

## How large was Ankylosaurus ?

Ankylosaurus was a massive, heavy animal. It grew to reach about 36 feet in length and stood almost 10 feet tall. Ankylosaurus weighed about 4 tons.

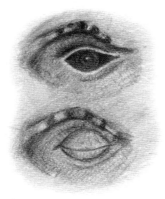

*Bony armor on the Ankylosaurus' legs formed more defense.*

## Could Ankylosaurus wink ?

The skull of Ankylosaurus was covered by sheets of bone armor. The eyes poked out through holes in the armor. The eyes would have been vulnerable to attack, but they were protected by armored eyelids covered with plates of bone. To protect its eyes, Ankylosaurus probably snapped them shut as if winking. In addition, when provoked, the body armor may have filled with blood and turned pink—meaning that it "blushed" too!

## What did Ankylosaurus eat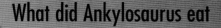

The teeth of Ankylosaurus were fairly small, and there were no teeth at all at the front of the mouth, where the animal had a sharp beak instead. Some scientists think that the Ankylosaurus ate fruits. Living in the same age and time as large hunters, such as Tyrannosaurus, and not possessing particularly effective fighting jaws, Ankylosaurus needed to find a way to protect itself by using its bony armor.

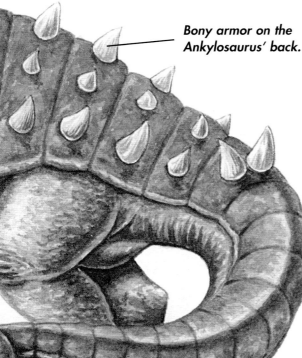

**Bony armor on the Ankylosaurus' back.**

**A large mass of solid bone formed the tail club.**

## How did it defend itself ?

Ankylosaurus had thick bone armor along its back, and if it was threatened, probably crouched down so that the unarmored legs and belly were protected. The bony plates and spikes protected nearly all of its body, even its eyes. The only way a predator would have been able to attack Ankylosaurus would have been to flip it over and attack its soft underbelly. Most would give up and look for easier prey!

## What did the tail club do ?

The end of the tail was equipped with a large mass of solid bone and the tail was linked to massively powerful muscles over the hips. Ankylosaurus probably used the bony mass as a dangerous club. It may have brandished the club to fight off attacking hunters.

### FACT BYTES

The ankylosaur family are commonly known as the "fused together lizards."

Ankylosaurus may have been one of the last dinosaurs to ever walk on Earth.

Ankylosaurus is sometimes called Euplocephalus, but it is now believed that these were two different animals.

**ANKYLOSAURUS**

# TRICERATOPS

The name Triceratops means "three-horned-face," and was given to this dinosaur because of the three sharp horns that grew from its skull. Since Triceratops was discovered, scientists have found several other dinosaurs which had three horns and were very like Triceratops.

## When, and where, did Triceratops live ?

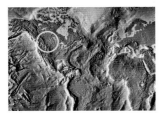

Triceratops, one of the last of the dinosaurs, lived at the end of the Cretaceous Period, in the Mesozoic Era which means "age of reptiles." Over 50 skulls and partial skeletons have been found, mainly in western Canada and the United States. Palaeontologist Othniel Marsh was the first to name Triceratops, in 1889—it was first thought to be an extinct species of buffalo!

| TRIASSIC 245–208 million years | JURASSIC 208–146 million years | CRETACEOUS 146–65 million years |
| --- | --- | --- |

## How many types of Triceratops were there ?

Scientists have found dozens of fossils of Triceratops. They have classified the fossils into nine different species of Triceratops based on the size and shape of the horns and the bone frill at the back of the skull. Some scientists think that these were not different types of Triceratops, but that individual Triceratops just adapted their bodies and behavior to suit different climates—much like the animals of today. The finding of new fossils may affect the way in which dinosaurs are classified. The discovery of a more complete skeleton would allow paleontologists to compare existing evidence, and what might have been thought of as three species of Triceratops (for example) may only prove to be one.

## Who was John Bell Hatcher ?

American scientist John Bell Hatcher was known as "The King of the Collectors" during the 1880s and 1890s. He went to Wyoming in 1889 to look for dinosaur fossils, and found a total of 50 ceratopsians, 30 of which were Triceratops. One of his finds contained the first skull to be discovered, and weighed almost 7,000 pounds! It had to be dragged to the railway by horse and cart. No one since has had such a successful find. He died of typhoid in 1904, and was buried in an unmarked grave. This was corrected in 1995.

## What dinosaur attacked Triceratops

Triceratops lived alongside powerful hunters such as Tyrannosaurus. One fossil of a Triceratops' skull was found which had bite marks on it. The marks matched those which would have been made by a Tyrannosaurus' jaw, a strong indication that Tyrannosaurus hunted Triceratops. Young Triceratops would have been easy to attack and it is thought that the adult Triceratops may have formed a ring around the young to protect them.

*Triceratops' neck frill was a solid sheet of bone.*

### FACT BYTES

Despite the facial similarities, an adult Triceratops would have been much bigger than our modern-day rhinoceros— standing at around 13 feet high and 30 feet long!

## How large was Triceratops

The biggest form of Triceratops was Triceratops horridus, which means "horrible three-horn face." This species grew to be 30 feet long and may have weighed 6 tons. It is similar in ways to our modern-day rhinoceros, which has horns growing forwards from its face. The legs were also fairly similar. Triceratops was probably able to move as fast as a modern rhinoceros and may have had a similar lifestyle.

# EXTINCTION

During the Mesozoic Era, millions of dinosaurs belonging to thousands of different species walked on Earth. They were the largest and most important animals on land. Today there are no living dinosaurs anywhere—they have all become extinct.

## When did dinosaurs become extinct ❓

Dinosaurs became extinct at the end of the Cretaceous Period, about 65 million years ago. They vanished from all the continents at the same time. As fossils can be dated to only the nearest million years or so, it is impossible to say if the extinction happened suddenly or was spread out over thousands of years. Once an animal has become extinct it cannot come back naturally.

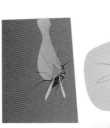

Blood-sucking insects, such as mosquitos, used to feed on the blood of dinosaurs, much as they feed on animals today. Sometimes these insects would get trapped in sticky tree resin. This resin would then harden and form amber with the insect preserved inside. One day, scientists may be able to re-create dinosaurs from the information contained in the DNA extracted from the blood once sucked by these prehistoric insects!

## What else became extinct ❓

Several other groups of animals vanished at the same time that dinosaurs became extinct. The flying reptiles, the pterosaurs, died out as did the sea reptiles. Several types of shellfish, reptiles and other animals also died out about the same time.

## Why do scientists suggest a giant asteroid ?

Scientist studying the rocks from the time the dinosaurs became extinct noticed that they contain large amounts of a chemical called iridium. Iridium is rare on Earth, but is common in asteroids. This suggests that a giant asteroid had hit Earth and exploded, scattering dust across the world! If the asteroid which hit Earth was big enough, about 10 miles across, it would have caused dust to fill the upper atmosphere. This would have blocked out the Sun's rays and plunged Earth into a long period of freezing darkness. This would have killed most plants and, without food, the dinosaurs would have died out.

## What animals survived the dinosaurs ?

*Dinosaur extinction was rather sudden. One theory as to why it happened speculates that a giant asteroid hit earth.*

There are no dinosaurs alive today and no fossils of dinosaurs have been found which date to after the end of the Cretaceous Period. It would seem that all the dinosaurs died out. However, a type of small theropod dinosaur had evolved into birds about 160 million years ago. These birds survived, so the descendants of dinosaurs did survive the extinction. After the dinosaurs became extinct, other types of animals took over the world. During the time of the dinosaurs, mammals had been small and rare. Now they have increased in number and rapidly evolved into many different types of animal. Today, it is the mammals which rule the world, as the dinosaurs once did.

*Descended from reptiles, mammals now rule the world.*

# GLOSSARY

**Allosaurus**
Hunted alone, as they were large enough to kill their prey unaided.

**Ambush**
The method by which some dinosaurs killed their prey—by hiding and then pouncing on it.

**Ancestor**
An early dinosaur, animal, plant, etc. from which a later type has developed.

**Ancient Greek**
A language used to identify objects and scientific principles in order that all Palaeontologists use the same terms.

**Ankylosaurus**
Covered in plates of armor, they walked on all four legs.

**Argentinosaurus**
The remains of this dinosaur make Palaeontologists believe this to be the biggest that ever existed.

**Baryonyx**
Believed to be a fish-eating dinosaur with long, thin teeth.

**Brachiosaurus**
A long-necked dinosaur that ate huge amounts of plants.

**Cannibal**
An animal which eats others of its own kind.

**Ceratopsians**
Horned plant-eaters with a beak and sharp, slicing teeth.

**Compsognathus**
A small, light-boned dinosaur with very sharp teeth.

**Crest**
A tall, thin structure found on top of the head of some dinosaurs.

**Cretaceous Period**
Began about 146 million years ago and ended about 65 million years ago. The third and last period of the Mesozoic Era.

**Deinonychus**
Known as "terrible claw," this dinosaur preferred to hunt in packs.

**Diapsid**
The group of reptiles to which all dinosaurs belong.

**Dravidosaurus**
A type of sea reptile whose fossils were originally thought to be of a stegosaur.

**Eoraptor**
This meat-eating dinosaur is believed to be one of the first to have existed.

**Evolve**
To develop and change gradually over long periods of time.

**Fossils**
The remains of animals or plants which have been found preserved in rocks.

**Giganotosaurus**
This dinosaur had the largest teeth—over 10 in. long.

**Hadrosaur**
A large family of ornithopod dinosaurs with distinctive bony crests on their skulls.

**Herd**
A group of plant-eating animals of the same type which live together most of the time.

**Hylaeosaurus**
The first ankylosaur to have been found, by scientist Richard Owen.

**Hypsilophodontids**
Small to medium ornithopods which walked on their hind legs.

**Ichthyosaur**
A type of sea reptile which lived at the time of the dinosaurs and looked rather like a giant fish.

**Iguanodon**
Meaning "iguana tooth," this dinosaur had a sidewards-sliding jaw.

**Jurassic Period**
Began about 200 million years ago and ended about 146 million years ago. The second period of the Mesozoic Era.

**Kentrosaurus**
A dinosaur with long spikes growing from its "shoulders."

**Latin**
The language used in ancient Rome and by present-day

Palaeontologists (see Ancient Greek).

**Mamenchisaurus**
These sauropods lived in China. They had the longest neck of any dinosaur discovered so far.

**Mesozoic**
Means "middle life."

**Mesozoic Era**
Began about 245 million years ago and ended about 65 million years ago.

**Missing Link**
The theory that a reptile existed that was a common ancestor of both the saurischia and ornithischia dinosaurs.

**Ornithischia**
One of the two main groups of dinosaurs with hip bones shaped like those of modern birds. All the ornithischia ate plants.

**Ornithomimosaurs**
These "bird-like" reptiles looked like present-day ostriches.

**Ornithopod**
A plant-eating dinosaur, whose name means "bird foot."

**Pachycephalosaur**
Meaning "thick skull reptile," this group of dinosaurs used to charge at each other using their skulls as protection.

**Pack**
A group of meat-eating animals of the same type which live together and help each other to hunt.

**Palaeontologists**
Scientists who study extinct animals and plants.

**Plates**
The pointed pieces of thinner bone sticking up from the back of dinosaurs such as Stegosaurus (see "Roof Reptiles").

**Plesiosaur**
A type of sea reptile which lived during the time of the dinosaurs.

**Polacanthus**
A dinosaur, believed to have lived in Britain some 125 million years ago.

**Pterosaur**
A type of flying reptile which lived during the time of the dinosaurs.

**Roof Reptiles**
A name given to stegosaurs, identified by their large bone plates and spikes which run along their backs.

**Saurischia**
One of the two main groups of dinosaurs formed of either meat- or plant eaters, all with hip bones shaped like those of modern lizards.

**Sauropods**
These enormous dinosaurs laid huge eggs—often larger than footballs!

**Scavenge**
To search through decaying or unwanted matter to find something to eat.

**Seismosaurus**
The longest dinosaur believed to have lived.

**Stegosaurs**
These dinosaurs were plant eaters, walking on four legs.

**Struthiomimus**
Supposedly the fastest dinosaur, with long muscular legs helping it to reach speeds of 45 mph.

**Styracosaurus**
A dinosaur with one forward-pointing horn and several others around the back of the skull.

**Tanganyika**
An area in Africa, now part of Tanzania.

**Triassic Period**
Began about 245 million years ago and ended about 200 million years ago. The first period of the Mesozoic Era.

**Triceratops**
Name of dinosaur meaning "three-horned face" because of the horns growing from its skull.

**Tuojiangosaurus**
One of the only dinosaurs believed to have lived in Japan.

# INDEX

Key: Top - t; middle - m; bottom - b; left - l; right -r.
Front and back cover: Meme Design, John Butler and Corel.
1: Meme Design*. 2: (tl) Meme Design*; (tr) Corel. 3: Meme Design*. 4: (tl) TTAT; (ml, bl) Meme Design*; (mr) Corel. 5: Meme Design*. 6: (ml, mr) Meme Design*; (b) John Butler. 7: (tr) Corel; (mr) John Butler. 8: (t) John Butler; (b) Meme Design*. 9: TTAT. 10: (ml,mr) Meme Design*; (bl) Robert Morton. 11: (mr) Corel; (br) John Butler. 12-16: Meme Design*. 17: (t) Meme Design*; (br) John Butler. 18: (t,br) Meme Design*; (bl) John Butler. 19: (t,m) Meme Design*; (br) Corel. 20: (t,m) Meme Design*; (b) John Butler. 21: (t,m) Meme Design*; (br) TTAT. 22: (t) Meme Design*; (bl) Robert Morton. 23–24: Meme Design*. 25: (t) NASA; (b) Meme Design*. 26-27: Meme Design*. 28: (t, mr) Meme Design*; (ml) Corel; (bl) Robert Morton. 29: (t,b) Meme Design*; (m) Topham Picturepoint/ImageWorks. 30: (bl) Robert Morton. 31: Meme Design*. 32: (t,m, br) Meme Design*; (bl) John Butler. 33: Meme Design*. 34: (t,m) Meme Design*; (b) Corel. 35: Meme Design*. 36: (t,m) Meme Design*; (b) Corel. 37: Meme Design*. 38: (t, mr) Meme Design*; (ml) John Butler. 39: Meme Design*. 40: (t, mr, b) Meme Design*; (ml) John Butler. 41: (tl) Robert Morton; (ml) Meme Design*; (mr) John Butler; (br) Corel. 42: Meme Design*. 43: (t,m) Meme Design*; (br) Corel. 44: Meme Design*. 45: (t) John Butler; (b) Digital Stock.          *Meme Design illustrations by Alex Head-Weston and Sarah Lever.